MY FIRST BOOK OF SOUNDS

GIANT TRUCKS

A PRESS & PLAY SOUND BOOK

APPLESAUCE PRESS

KENNEBUNKPORT, MAINE

Cur-CLUNK! BULLDOZERS CAN PUSH AND DUMP ALL KINDS OF MATERIALS.

THEY HAVE A LARGE CLAW ON THE BACK THAT CAN RIP APART ROCK AND EARTH.

MAGIC TOUCH PAGE
PRESS HERE

What sound does an EXCAVATOR make?

Gr Gr k K GRK!
EXCAVATORS DIG TRENCHES AND HOLES

EXCAVATORS HAVE A BIG ARM TO SCOOP UP HEAVY THINGS.

MAGIC TOUCH PAGE
PRESS HERE

What sound does a DUMP TRUCK make?

CRASH!
DUMP TRUCKS HAVE AN OPEN-BOX BED THAT TIPS OVER.

THEY CARRY DIRT, SAND, GRAVEL, AND MORE.

MAGIC TOUCH PAGE
PRESS HERE

What does an **AMBULANCE** siren sound like?

Wee woo! Wee woo!
AMBULANCES HELP PEOPLE IN EMERGENCIES AND TAKE THEM TO THE HOSPITAL.

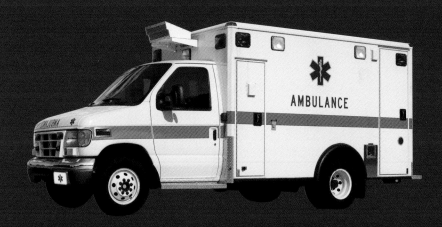

AMBULANCES HAVE SPECIAL EQUIPMENT AND MEDICINE TO HELP SICK OR INJURED PEOPLE.

COUNTY EMERGENCY MEDICAL SERVICE

141-M3

What sound does a CRANE make?

Ch-ch-ch-ch-ch! CRANES LIFT AND LOWER MATERIALS. THEY HAVE A LONG ARM WITH ROPES OR CHAINS TO HOIST HEAVY THINGS.

THEY ARE USED FOR CONSTRUCTION WORK AND FOR LOADING TRAINS AND SHIPS.

MAGIC TOUCH PAGE

♪

PRESS HERE

What does a **SCHOOL BUS** horn sound like?

BEEP, BEEP! SCHOOL BUSES TAKE STUDENTS TO SCHOOL. THEY HAVE ROWS OF SEATS TO FIT LOTS OF PEOPLE.

SCHOOL BUSES HAVE A STOP SIGN SO KIDS CAN GET ON AND OFF SAFELY.

SCHOOL BUS

MAGIC TOUCH PAGE ♪ PRESS HERE

What sound does a GARBAGE TRUCK make?

Cr-CRASH!
GARBAGE TRUCKS PICK UP TRASH FROM HOMES AND BUSINESSES. SOME PICK UP RECYCLING TOO!

THEY CAN LOAD GARBAGE FROM THE FRONT, SIDE, OR BACK.

CAUTION
VEHICLE STOPS AND BACKS FREQUENTLY

CAUTION
WIDE
RIGHT
TURNS
DO NOT PASS
ON RIGHT

MAGIC TOUCH PAGE
PRESS HERE

What sound does a ROAD ROLLER make?

Cr-CRUSH!

ROAD ROLLERS COMPACT CONCRETE, ASPHALT, SOIL, OR GRAVEL TO MAKE ROADS. THEY HAVE BIG METAL DRUMS TO HELP FLATTEN SURFACES.

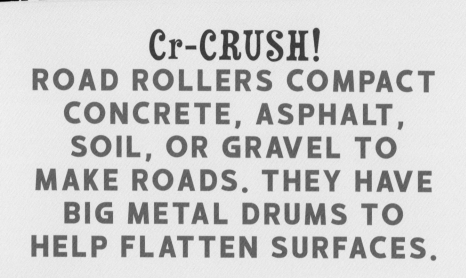

ROAD ROLLERS ARE VERY HEAVY, THEY WEIGH ABOUT 40,000 POUNDS!

MAGIC TOUCH PAGE

♪

PRESS HERE

What sound does a TOW TRUCK make?

Vroom, vroom!
TOW TRUCKS MOVE CARS THAT ARE BROKEN DOWN OR STUCK.

TOW TRUCKS PULL CARS ONTO A FLATBED WITH A WINCH.

MAGIC TOUCH PAGE
PRESS HERE

What does a FIRE ENGINE siren sound like?

Eeeooooeeeooo!
FIRE ENGINES ARE USED BY FIREFIGHTERS TO FIGHT FIRES. FIREFIGHTERS USE THE LADDERS AND HOSES.

FIRE ENGINES CARRY LOTS OF WATER TO HELP PUT OUT FIRES.

What does a BIG RIG horn sound like?

Honk, honk! BIG RIGS PULL TRAILERS THAT CARRY CARGO.

BIG RIGS ARE DRIVEN ACROSS THE COUNTRY TO DELIVER GOODS.

MAGIC TOUCH PAGE
PRESS HERE

What sound does a SNOWPLOW make?

Sc-scrape!
SNOWPLOWS REMOVE SNOW FROM THE ROAD. THEY HAVE A BIG BLADE THAT THEY USE TO MOVE SNOW AND ICE.

THEY CLEAR THE WAY FOR OTHER CARS AND TRUCKS TO DRIVE AFTER A STORM.